# The Story of Me

Designed for Parents to Read to Their Child
at Ages 3 Through 5

## BY STAN AND BRENNA JONES

Illustrated by Joel Spector

**NAVPRESS** ◐
BRINGING TRUTH TO LIFE
NavPress Publishing Group
P.O. Box 35001, Colorado Springs, Colorado 80935

The Navigators is an international Christian organization. Jesus Christ gave His followers the Great Commission to go and make disciples (Matthew 28:19). The aim of The Navigators is to help fulfill that commission by multiplying laborers for Christ in every nation.

NavPress is the publishing ministry of The Navigators. NavPress publications are tools to help Christians grow. Although publications alone cannot make disciples or change lives, they can help believers learn biblical discipleship, and apply what they learn to their lives and ministries.

Library of Congress Catalog Card Number:
94-67288
ISBN 08910-98437

Cover and interior illustrations: Joel Spector

Printed in the United States of America

3 4 5 6 7 8 9 10 11 12 13 14 15 / 99 98 97 96 95

To Lindsay

## Acknowledgments

We wish to thank the editorial, production, and marketing staffs of NavPress, especially Steve Webb, for their support of this project. Cathy Davis provided immensely valuable feedback as our consulting children's editor; *What's the Big Deal? Why God Cares About Sex* and *Facing the Facts: The Truth About Sex and You* especially benefited from her insights and editing skills. Our thanks go out to Sanna Baker and Carolyn Nystrom for reading and commenting on the early drafts of *The Story of Me*, and to Lisa, Mark, and Anna McMinn for reading and commenting on the early drafts of *What's the Big Deal?* Finally, our thanks to Carol Blauwkamp for help with typing parts of the early drafts of several of these books.

# General Introduction to the GOD'S DESIGN FOR SEX Children's Book Series

This book is one of a series designed to help parents shape their children's character, particularly in the area of sexuality. From their earliest years, our children are bombarded constantly with destructive and false messages about the nature of sexuality and the place of sexual intimacy in life through the media, discussions with their friends, and school sex-education programs. The result? Skyrocketing rates of teen sexual activity, pregnancy, abortion, sexually transmitted diseases, divorce, and devastated lives.

Our conclusion from studying this crisis, the nature of human sexuality, and most importantly, the Scriptures is that *our God wants Christian parents to be the primary sex educators of their children.* And if we are going to have a powerful impact, we must start early, working to lay a godly foundation of understanding of their sexuality before the twisted ideas of the world have a chance to take root. First messages are the most powerful; why wait until your child hears the wrong thing and then try to correct the misunderstanding? God made sexuality, and He made it as a beautiful gift; why not present it to our children the way God intended?

Our first book, *How and When to Tell Your Kids About Sex: A Lifelong Approach to Shaping Your Child's Sexual Character* (NavPress, 1993), was designed to provide parents with a comprehensive understanding of what they can do to shape their child's "sexual character." Some of our specific goals in that book were to:

- help you understand your role in shaping your child's views, attitudes, and beliefs about sexuality;
- help you understand and shape the building blocks of your child's character;
- clarify what God's view of our sexuality is;
- discuss how to explain and defend the traditional Christian view of sexual morality in these modern times;
- explore how you can most powerfully influence your child to make a decision for sexual abstinence (chastity); and
- equip you, the parent, to provide your child with the strengths necessary to stand by his or her commitments to traditional Christian morality.

In *How and When to Tell Your Kids About Sex* we provided numerous dialogues between parents and children at different ages, and offered many suggestions about how difficult subjects could be approached. Nevertheless, the most frequent comment we heard from parents who read our book was, "I really think you are right, but I don't think I can talk to my child that way. I wish there was something we could read with our children to get us started in discussing these matters." The books in this series are designed to meet that need.

For the sake of this children's book series, we have divided the years between birth and puberty into four time periods. We have made these periods overlap because there are differences in children's maturity levels that only you as a parent can know; there are eight-year-olds who are more mature than some ten-year-olds, for example. The broad age ranges we have used are: three to five, five to eight, eight to eleven, and eleven to fourteen. We have written one book for each age range.

The first three of these four books are designed to be read *by parents to their children*. They are not, by themselves, meant to provide all of the information that kids need. They are to be *starting points* for you, the Christian parent, to discuss sexuality with your children in a manner appropriate to each age. They provide an anchor point for discussions, a jump-start to get discussions going. We suggest that you not simply hand these books to your child to read, because *it is how you as a parent handle the issue of sexuality that will have the greatest impact upon your child*. The fourth book is designed to be read by the child, now eleven to fourteen years in age, but we hope parents will also read the book and discuss its contents with the child.

## Book One (Ages Three to Five): The Story of Me

Our most important task with a young child is to lay a spiritual *foundation* for the child's understanding of his or her sexuality. Book one helps you do that. It is vital that our children see their bodies and their sexuality (their "girl-ness" or "boy-ness") for what it is: a gift from God, a *marvelous* gift. They must see that God made their bodies on purpose, that God loves the human body (and the whole human person), and that God regards it as a work of divine art that in the beginning He called "very good" (Genesis 1:31). They must see that God loves women and men evenly; both are created in the image of God. Children must see not only their bodies, not only their existence as boys or girls, but also their sexual organs as a gift from God. They can begin to develop an appreciation for God's marvelous gift by understanding some of the basics of human reproduction, and so the growth of a child inside a mother's body and the birth process are discussed in this book. It is critical that children at this age begin to develop a trust for God's Law and see God as a lawgiver who has the best interests of His people at heart. Finally, it is critical at this stage that children come to see families as God's intended framework for the nurture and love of children. We hope you will find *The Story of Me* a wonderful starting point for discussing sexuality with your young child.

### Book Two (Ages Five to Eight): Before I Was Born (by Carolyn Nystrom)

Building upon the topics in book one, Carolyn Nystrom further emphasizes the creational goodness of our bodies, our existence as men and women, and our sexual organs. New topics are introduced as well. The book discusses growth and change in a boy's body as he becomes a man, and in a girl's body as she becomes a woman. Tactfully and directly, it explains the basic nature of sexual intercourse between a husband and wife. Undergirding this information is the foundation of Christian morality: that God wants sexual intercourse limited to marriage because it brings a husband and wife together in a way that honors God and helps build strong families. This foundation will be vitally important later in the life of your child.

It is not uncommon for parents to ask, "Do my kids really need to know about sexual intercourse this early?" The answer is yes. First, there is no good rationale for keeping kids ignorant about this basic area of life. We must remember that the Hebrew people, in and through whom God revealed His divine will, were farmers and ranchers among whom the breeding of animals was part of everyday life. Further, their culture was one with much less privacy than we have today. Homes were small, without glass for windows or stereos for background noise, and three or more generations commonly lived together. It was in the context of a society steeped in what we politely call "animal husbandry," a society with little privacy and definite "earthy" attitudes toward sexuality, that our Lord's will and rules about sexuality were revealed. We don't need to shelter our kids by keeping them "in the dark."

The second reason for telling your kids about sexual intercourse early is that positive, first messages are always the most powerful. Our children are exposed to the facts about sexual intercourse on the playgrounds of their schools and in the backyards of our neighborhoods. If we want to shape godly attitudes in our children about sex, why would we wait until they soak in the errors and misperceptions of the world and then try to change their attitudes? Why not instead build from the foundation up?

### Book Three (Ages Eight to Eleven): What's the Big Deal? Why God Cares About Sex

This book attempts to do three things. First, it attempts to review and reinforce the messages of the first two books: the basics of sexual intercourse and the fundamental creational goodness of our sexuality.

Second, it attempts to continue the task of explicitly and deliberately building your child's understanding of why God intends sexual intercourse to be reserved for marriage.

Third, this book will attempt to help you begin the process of "inoculating" your child against the negative moral messages of the world. In *How and When to Tell Your Kids About Sex* we argue that Christian parents should *not* try to shelter their children from all of the destructive moral messages of the secular world. When we shelter them, we leave them naive and vulnerable, and we risk communicating that these negative messages are so powerful that Christians cannot deal with them. Too much sheltering will leave our children defenseless against the attacks they will receive from the world.

But neither should we just let our kids be inundated with destructive messages. The principle of inoculation suggests that we gently expose our kids to the contrary moral messages they will soon hear anyway. It should be in our *homes* that our kids first learn that many people in our world do not believe in reserving sex for marriage, as well as getting their first understanding of such problems as teenage pregnancy, AIDS, and so forth. But they should be exposed to these realities *for a vital purpose*, so that we parents can help build their defenses against these terrible problems of our culture. In doing so, we can strengthen their resolve to stand by the traditional Christian ethic and send them into the world prepared to defend their beliefs and choices.

### Book Four (Ages Eleven to Fourteen): Facing the Facts: The Truth About Sex and You

*Facing the Facts: The Truth About Sex and You* will attempt again to build upon all that has come before, but will prepare your child for puberty in more depth. Your child is now old enough for more detailed information about the changes her or his body is about to go through, and about the adult body that is soon to be presented to her or him as a gift from God. Your child also needs to be reminded about God's view of sexuality, about His loving and beautiful intentions for how this gift should be used. The distorted ways in which our world views sex must be clearly labeled, and our children must be prepared to face views and beliefs contrary to those we are teaching them at home. We attempt to do all this while also talking about the many confusing feelings of puberty and early adolescence. We hope that our talking about these feelings will encourage loving conversation between you and your developing children as they go through this challenging period. This book is meant to be read by the child himself or herself, but we urge you to read it too, and then talk about it with your child.

All of these books were written as if dialogue were an ongoing reality between a child, his or her mother and father, and other siblings in the home. Yet in some homes only one parent is willing to talk about sex; in others only one of two parents is a Christian. Many Christian parents are not in intact, two-parent, "traditional" homes. We hope these books will be used by and be useful to single parents, grandparents who are the primary care-givers to a child or children, parents with just one child, adoptive or foster parents, and other families that do not fit the "traditional" mold. Obviously, use of these books by "nontraditional" families will require some special creativity and thought. But this is really no different from the challenges you face in talking about sex with your child in the first place. Sex education is hard when you do not have a partner who can share the other gender's perspective, when an absent partner is not a good role model, or when discussion of the topic raises painful memories and unresolved issues. We are concerned about these challenges but urge you *to press onward anyway*. The welfare of your child requires that you address the issues raised in these books. Better that they be addressed constructively and directly than left to fester unexplored.

Thank you for trusting us to help you in this great adventure of shaping your child's sexual character. We hope these books will be valuable tools in raising a new generation of faithful Christian young people who will have healthy, positive, accepting attitudes about their own sexuality; who will live confident, chaste lives as faithful witnesses to the work of Christ in their lives while they are single, and then fulfilled, loving, rewarding lives as spouses.

Remember that what you tell your child about sexuality is only part of the puzzle. How you live your lives as parents before your children will have the greatest impact upon them. Teenagers who have a close relationship with a parent are better prepared to resist sexual temptation and pressure than those who are disconnected from their parents; work on having a loving, caring, listening, supportive relationship with your teens. Encourage their own unique, independent relationship with the living God by family church attendance, by prayer and study of the Scriptures individually and as a family, and by the ways in which you live your everyday lives (Deuteronomy 6:1-9). Prayerfully send them out into the world, and always be available as a model of God's love, discipline, and forgiveness.

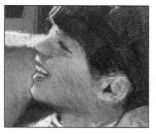

**Tell me my story again, Daddy!**

**Okay. You're Paul Pettijohn, you're 4 and 1/2, and you live at 4412 Comet Road, Apartment 3-B, in....**

**No, No! I don't mean that! I mean tell me where I came from! Tell me the story about ME!**

**Oh, THAT story! We would be glad to! Mommy, why don't you start it?**

 All right. . . . Long ago, God knew all about our mommies and daddies, and their mommies and daddies, and theirs and theirs. . . . He knew about your father and me, and your sister and you. And He already loved us all! One reason God made Daddy and me is so we would love each other, and have you and Sarah and love you both.

 Was that why I was born? So that you would have a little boy to love?

Yes, and for other reasons, too! God wants you to love Him with your whole heart, now and when you grow to be a man. God also has some important work for you to do, maybe to be a father yourself. And God wants others to know more about Jesus by the way you live your life. When you obey God's rules and live like Jesus, other people will know more about God from watching you!

 And how did God make me, Daddy? First, He started by having you and Mommy love each other and then. . . .

That's right! First, a man and a woman should love each other and get married. God wants only people who are married to have babies. Having a baby to take care of is hard work. A little boy or little girl needs a lot of love. When a mommy and daddy are married, they can both give their child lots of love; just the right amount. They both have special kinds of love to give.

Was I in Mommy's tummy right away when you got married?

No, God waited a couple of years. Then He took a tiny piece of Daddy's body and a tiny piece of Mommy's body, and made YOU! That is why you look a little like me and a little like Mommy. But you were too tiny to live out in this world. So God put you in Mommy's womb, or uterus, inside her body. That is a special place made just to protect God's little ones. It is a place to grow until you are big enough to hug and feed and play with! It takes about nine months to grow that big.

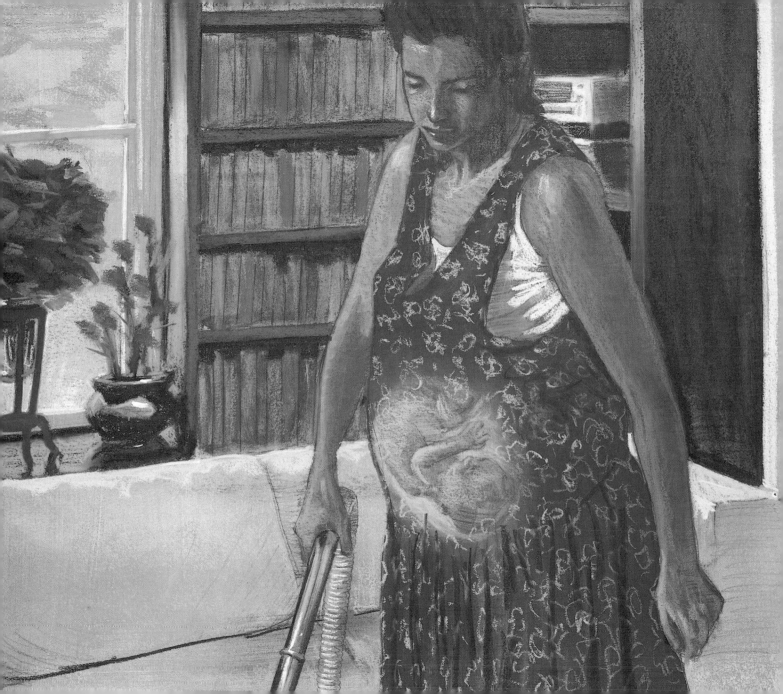

 But how could I breathe inside of Mommy? And how could I get anything to eat?

Ah! Those are great questions! God takes care of that by the way that He makes each little baby and the way He makes mommies. God makes babies so that every one has an umbilical cord. It's like a hose through which the baby can get food and water and air from the mommy. The food and water and air are in tiny little pieces and pass from the mommy's blood right into the baby's blood. So the baby doesn't have to breathe or eat or drink, but still gets all of the water and food and air it needs!

 Mommy, is that why I have a bellybutton?

That's right! That is where your cord connected from your tummy to the inside of my womb. So while you were growing in my tummy from the size of a little piece of sand to being big enough to come out, you got all of the air, water, and food you needed through your bellybutton. And you must have liked what you were getting, because you sure did grow big! My tummy really stuck out a lot!

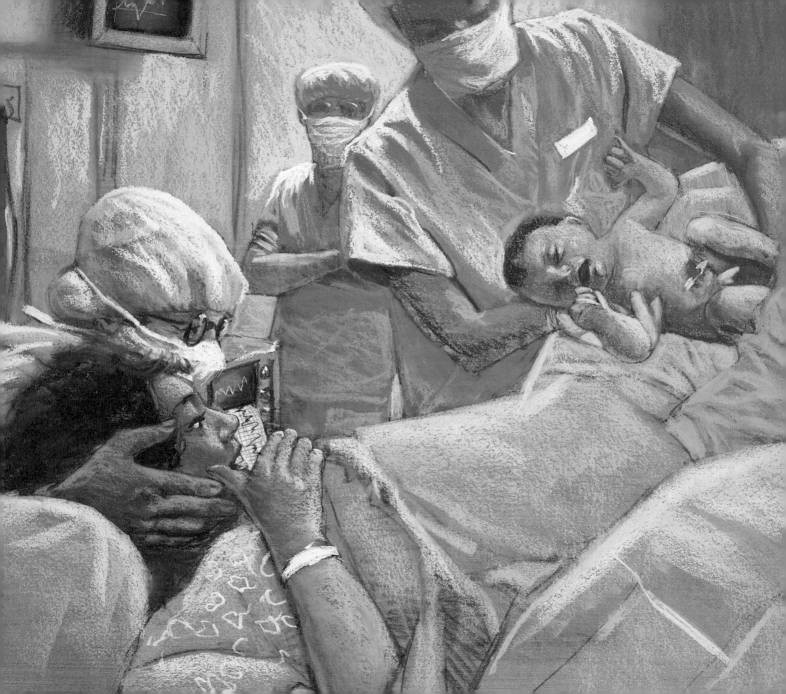

 Did your tummy get as big with me as it did with Sarah? That big?

It did! And when the time was right, you came out into the world through my vagina. The muscles pushed really hard. God made my vagina so that it could stretch just big enough to let you out. Daddy got to watch you being born, and it was like a miracle for him to see you come from inside my body!

But Sarah didn't come out that way, did she, Daddy?

No, Sarah was upside-down in Mommy's womb. The doctor decided to operate, to open Mommy's tummy to let Sarah out safely. Neither Mommy or Sarah would have been safe if the doctor had tried to let Sarah be born through Mommy's vagina. It hurt a bit, but we were so glad to have Sarah out safely and for your Mommy to be okay.

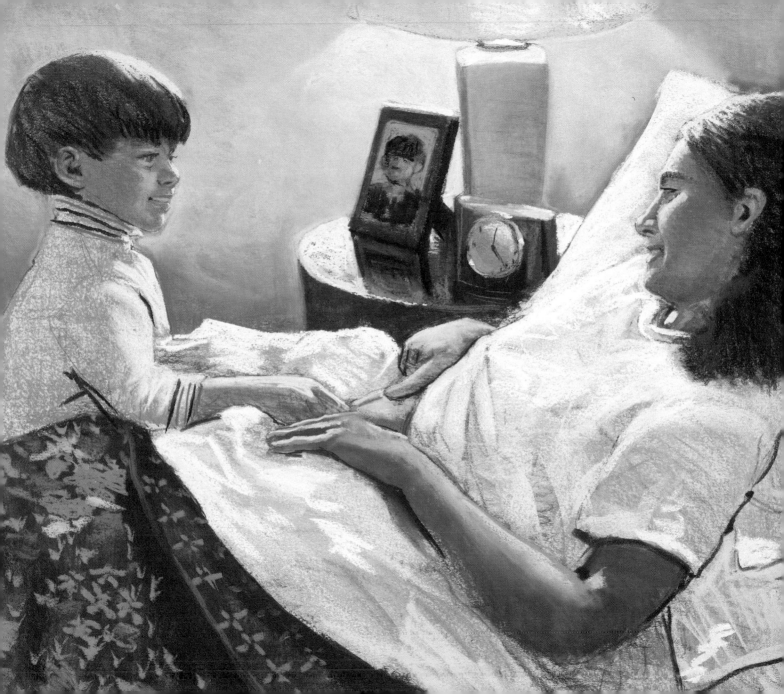

 What was I like when I was a baby?

You were tiny; about this big! You had the most perfect little arms, feet, eyes, nose.... The doctor saw right away that you had a penis, and that's how she knew you were a boy! And you had brown eyes, and dark, dark hair—you were beautiful. We loved you before you were born, and we loved you even more when we got to hold you.

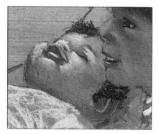 I have a penis, but Sarah doesn't. That makes me a boy like Daddy. I'm glad I'm a boy!

I am, too, and so is God! He made you special. Girls are special too. God gave Sarah a vagina and a womb, and He didn't give that to you. That makes her a girl. Only girls can become mommies, and only boys can become daddies. Being a boy *or* a girl is special to God!

 But why, Mommy? Why did God make boys and girls?

God made all people to love God and make Him happy by obeying His rules. He wants people to live good lives. In the Bible, God tells the story of how He made the world. After He worked hard to make the earth, stars, oceans, plants, and animals, God said that all He had made was "good." But on the day God made the first man and the first woman, God said they were "very good!"

 Why? Because the man and woman made God really happy?

Yes. They made God very happy because they loved Him and loved each other. The Bible says that God is love. It also teaches that every family that is full of love is like a good picture on this earth of God's love. We can show we love each other by hugs and kisses, and by taking care of each other. A little boy like you can show Daddy and me you love us by obeying us, just like Daddy and I try to show God we love Him by obeying all of His rules. All of God's rules are good rules!

But are all hugs and kisses good, Daddy?

No, they are not all good. If you do not want to share a kiss or a hug or a touch with someone, you don't have to. God made you very special. He does not want anyone to take love from you that you don't want to share. And God made your body private. Mommy and I still help you take a bath, and a doctor might check every part of your body, but except for that your penis and a girl's vagina are private. Someday when you marry, your wife will be the only person you won't have to be private with at all.

 And is that when I might become a daddy?

Yes, if God blesses you that way. And we sure hope He will!

Mommy, will my wife give our baby milk from her breasts like you do to Sarah?

Yes, she will be able to. It's wonderful the way God made women's bodies. Mothers' bodies take the food we eat and make part of it into milk that comes out of our breasts. Our milk is the perfect food for a young baby! Women's bodies are amazing, and so are boys' bodies, each in different ways.

 I love that story! I love to know how God made me!

It is a wonderful story, Paul. It is one of the most wonderful stories there is.